Real Outreach
A Practical Guide to Retaining and Graduating College Students

By Ezella McPherson, Ph.D.

Written by: Ezella McPherson © 2021

Printed in the United States of America

ISBN: 978-0-578-89382-2

Dr. McPherson Coaching LLC
Detroit, Michigan
www.drmcphersoncoaching.com

Library of Congress Control Number: 2021907756

1.College Students **2.** Higher Education Administration
3. Academic Development Counseling **4.** Self Help **5.** Student Success **6.** Motivational **7.** College Graduation **8.** Adult and Continuing Education

Table of Contents

Dedication

This book is dedicated to everyone who desires to make a difference in the lives of college students to help facilitate their retention and graduation. You inspire all of us to be change agents in the lives of our students.

Preface

Although higher education institutions are making great strides toward enrolling students in college, retention and graduation of students remain a challenge. Student retention begins when students enter the university at orientation, continues each term as their studies continue, and ends when the students graduate. There are multiple reasons why some students stay in college while other students leave. However, few scholars or practitioners have written practical guides about successful retention and graduation programs or models.

As a student retention and graduation expert, I have designed a practical guide to help administrators, faculty members, staff, students, and families understand the ongoing needs of college students to help students not only persist in their studies but also graduate from college. The book begins with my story and retention experience. Following that, each chapter outlines a key component of a resource to support and facilitate student retention and graduation. These key support systems include academic advisors, academic success coaches, mentors, student organizations, employment opportunities, and technology. I also discuss the importance of creating a paper trail and report writing. The final chapter outlines a strategic approach that I use to support college students. I call this successful retention and graduation model *Real Outreach*.

Chapter 1
My Story and Retention Experience

I am an African American woman first-generation college graduate. I was afforded the opportunity to attend my first college choice, the University of Michigan (U of M)–Ann Arbor, for my undergraduate degree. I attended the U of M Residential College during my freshman year, which allowed me to take smaller classes with my peers in the East Quadrangle dorm. During my freshman year, my first assigned reading was a nearly 400-page book entitled *A Hope in the Unseen: An American Odyssey from the Inner City to the Ivy League*. The book tells the story of an African American man, Cedric Jennings, from Washington, DC. He was admitted to and chose to attend the prestigious Brown University. He faced academic and social challenges, yet he persevered and graduated from college.

Like Cedric Jennings, I faced academic challenges in college. I remember going to the U of M Sweetland Writing Center to get my papers critiqued because my first-year writing professor was convinced that I lacked "college writing skills." In addition, I had not participated in the U of M Summer Bridge Scholars Program, a program that is designed to provide academic and social support to students prior to their freshman year of college. However, I did use the supplemental services provided by the U of M Literature, Science, and the Arts (LSA) Comprehensive Studies Program, including an academic advisor and tutoring. I attended professors' office hours as needed to better understand assignments and to build relationships with my professors. I also had the benefit of having a good academic advisor at the U of M College of LSA.

In addition to academic challenges, I also endured financial challenges in college. As an out-of-state college student, I owed money each term until I moved off campus. During the end of my freshman year, I obtained a $750 scholarship from the U of M Oklahoma Alumni Association, which allowed me to pay off the rest of my tuition bill and have a great holiday season. In my second year of college, tuition at the U of M was raised, and once again, I owed money. I worked two jobs my sophomore year; one was at the U of M Office of Student Activities and Leadership, and the other was in the dining hall at the East Quadrangle, my place of residence at the time. Unfortunately, I had to quit the dining hall job by the middle of the winter semester of my sophomore year because it was affecting my academics. I just could not balance two jobs and complete my studies, so, I decided to be courageous and ask family members, an uncle and aunt in Detroit, for $300 to pay off my tuition bill. They were hesitant at first, but they agreed to loan me the money. I paid them back nearly a year later with the income tax refund I received during my junior year of college.

My aunt was dissatisfied that she had to loan me money to pay for college because she knew the U of M had funding for college students. She went to the U of M Financial Aid Office to advocate for me to obtain more funds due to the adversities that I was facing while in college, including my parents' separation and the loss of my home, among other life issues. I watched as my aunt advocated on my behalf for funding. I could not have done that kind of advocacy on my own behalf because I was a first-generation college student who did not know how to ask a financial aid counselor for additional funding. I was humbled and honored to obtain some funding for college.

My U of M financial aid counselor understood my financial needs and life issues, so she made sure that I obtained more funding, in addition to the federal grants (such as the Pell Grant) that I received, in the form of scholarships because I was doing well academically in the face of adversity. In my junior year, I received two new scholarships, the Michigan Achievement Award and the William L. Cooper Scholarship. During my senior year of college, I applied for and received a U of M LSA scholarship. Thus, by my last year in college, I needed fewer loans to pay for college compared to my freshman year.

However, financial and academic challenges were not the only challenges I confronted in college. I also faced mental challenges, namely grief. At one point, I went to the U of M Counseling and Psychological Services to seek help dealing with grief after my grandmother passed away. I was told by the counselor to "drop out of college" after I mentioned my grief and life issues. As I reflect on that experience, I realize that my counselor was not culturally competent, nor did she understand the power of mentoring, caring, and resiliency. That was one of the experiences that inspired me to mentor and encourage mentees and students facing adversity throughout their academic careers to stick to the course even in the face of adversity.

In contrast to my negative counseling experience, I had a strong group of friends, a work family, and mentors who supported me throughout my undergraduate journey. My work-study job was especially meaningful. I worked at the former U of M Office of Student Activities and Leadership, affectionately known as SAL. There, I connected students to student organizations during Festifall and Winterfest. I also helped award the Michigan Leadership Awards to student leaders and distributed pamphlets to students who wanted to start new organizations. Not only did this work-study job facilitate my own retention, but it also introduced me to student organizations, which are important tools to support student retention.

Despite the obstacles that I faced at the U of M due to academics, finances, and life issues, I earned my bachelor's degree. At the time, it was one of my greatest accomplishments because I was the first in my immediate family to earn a college degree. I did not stop there. I went on to obtain a master's degree and then a doctorate degree in educational policy studies.

At the University of Illinois, I worked in multiple positions where I learned about students' needs, including as a teaching assistant, graduate advisor, and research supervisor. Although I encouraged students to come to office hours, I saw few students during those hours. I met with most students after lectures and discussion sections. It was then I realized that students have busy lives.

At one point, I worked as a graduate advisor in the Access and Achievement Program (AAP) at the University of Illinois. The AAP provides students with the tools to be successful in obtaining a bachelor's degree. Without such support, the students might not be able to acquire a college degree. It was as a graduate advisor in the AAP that I gained a deeper understanding of the issues facing women of color by meeting with them one-on-one at a predominantly White institution.

In my first-year cohort in the AAP, I helped retain 86% of the women of color from the first year to the second year. In my second-year cohort, I did even better, retaining 100% of the women of color from their first year to their second year of college. Ninety-one percent of the women of color whom I worked with graduated from college. I also worked with African American students in the Ethnographic Research Lab headed by Dr. Robin Jarrett, an African American woman professor. There, I helped retain and graduate 100% of the students from the research lab.

In the tough 2012 economy, I landed my first position as an undergraduate academic advisor at Wayne State University. There, I worked with Engineering Bridge Program students. These were students who had not yet been fully admitted to a specific engineering program. They were required to take specialized courses (e.g., math and chemistry), and if they passed those courses, they were then admitted to a specific engineering program. I helped retain 87% of the Engineering Bridge Program students from fall 2012 to winter 2013. I worked with undecided engineering students as well. I retained 80% of those students from fall 2012 to winter 2013.

In the fall of 2013, I began working with the pre–electrical engineering and electrical engineering students. The pre–electrical engineering students were in their freshman or sophomore year of college and were enrolled in the lower-level electrical engineering curriculum. The electrical engineering students took the upper-level electrical engineering curriculum. They were declared students on track to graduate with a Bachelor of Science degree in electrical engineering. From the fall of 2013 to the fall of 2014, I retained 95% of declared electrical engineering majors and 84% of undeclared electrical engineering undergraduate students. I certified multiple degrees. However, what stood out most was certifying the Bachelor of Science degrees in electrical engineering of seven African American electrical engineering students (six males and one female) in 1 year.

In the winter of 2015, I was called to take on the role of inaugural director of the Indiana University (IU) South Bend Titan Success Center. The new center launched in the fall of 2015 because the team wanted to learn more about the campus dynamics and how we fit within the university. We introduced two new outreach initiatives in the fall of 2015; the first-year check-in and the IU Flags initiative. The first-year check-in program was a signature program that I personally designed for academically at-risk students who entered the university as conditionally admitted students. Typically, these students entered the university with a high school grade point average (GPA) of 2.4 or lower. With the help of a team of success coaches, 83% of program participants in the fall 2016 cohort returned for the spring 2017 term. Of the spring 2017 cohort, 75% of program participants persisted to the fall 2017 term with the support of success coaches and campus partners.

The IU Flags program was another academic support and early alert program. This program was for students who were flagged for issues such as attendance, course participation, missing assignments, and class performance. With the support of academic success coaches and campus partners, 69% of the fall 2016 IU Flags program participants returned for the spring 2017 term.

Another academic support program that I personally designed was the sophomore review program. The purpose of this program was to provide support to sophomore students in the fall 2016 term who had GPAs of 2.4 or below. With the support of academic success coaches and campus partners, 78% of the students who participated in this program returned for the spring 2017 term.

Although my time in the field of higher education ended in the fall of 2017, I am still passionate about the persistence, retention, and graduation of college students. In 2021 and beyond, I am committed to serving as a consultant to help higher education professionals, practitioners, and colleges and universities reach their college student retention and graduation goals.

Chapter 2

Academic Advising

An academic advisor is someone who is knowledgeable about the course curriculum, policies, and procedures within the university. Academic advisors also help students with choosing courses. They help students with their major curriculum by documenting their academic progress, and they complete degree audits as well. Academic advisors can go beyond advising by providing students with campus resource sheets. The campus offices on the resource sheet might include the Career Services Office, Office of Student Financial Aid, Student Accessibilities Services, Student Counseling Center, Student Success Center, and Tutoring Center.

Academic advisors can also provide students with grade point average (GPA) booster classes to help students raise their GPAs. GPA booster classes are courses that are relatively easy for students and in which they are likely to earn an A or B grade. These courses help students gain academic confidence throughout the term.

Finally, academic advisors can help students balance their schedules by learning students' strengths and weaknesses in terms of academic subjects. Past performance in courses may help an academic advisor determine whether a student can take courses that require heavy reading, multiple papers, and/or heavy quiz and exam loads.

As an academic advisor, to help students be successful, it is important to complete early outreach initiatives if they are not already being done on your college campus. Early outreach initiatives can entail working with your institution's institutional research team to pull data on students' progress prior to the midterm. Alternatively, you can pull students' grades using technology at your institution. At one of my institutions, I pulled DFWs (which stands for D, F, and withdrawal [W]) for courses within an institutional database.

For the early outreach initiative at one institution, I identified 66 students who had D and F grades within the first 4 to 6 weeks of the semester. I met one-on-one with some of those students to discuss their academic performance in their courses. I also connected students to campus resources, helped them with time management, and provided them with study tip sheets. Of the 28 students with whom I met, 20 (71%) remained in good standing and 8 (29%) were placed on academic probation. On the other hand, of the 38 students who failed to meet with me, 25 students (66%) were placed on academic probation and 13 (34%) remained in good academic standing. My early outreach efforts showed that college students can change their academic grades by the end of the term.

Larry was one early outreach student I met with at one of my institutions. He was an African American male and a first-generation college student from a low-income family. During our first meeting, I could tell he was feeling discouraged. He told me he was ready to drop out of college because of his slow academic progress. He was getting D and F grades on the early

14

academic assessments for three out of five engineering courses. In another meeting, he told me of a relative with terminal cancer and another family member who had just been diagnosed with cancer.

Larry left our meetings feeling empowered and inspired to continue his education. He passed all of his classes. Factors that contributed to Larry's success were the early alert system and grades reported by faculty members. We also created a student success plan that included participating in study groups and using campus resources. I shared with Larry a personal story of when I was in graduate school and my grandfather and aunt, who both had cancer, were given only a certain amount of time to live and how that was particularly difficult for me. However, I persevered despite obstacles, including a peer who declined to work with me on a class project. I had to work alone on the project, but I completed it. I believe that my story resonated with Larry. He was not alone in his academic journey while dealing with grief. The next semester, Larry told me that his relative had passed away from cancer. I encouraged him to stick with the course, and he did. He remained in school and completed all of his engineering classes. Larry eventually completed his Bachelor of Science degree in electrical engineering.

Another example of a student I advised was a Latina student named Adriana. She was on academic probation. She both worked and attended school. However, her high school did not fully prepare her for the rigors of college. She had not mastered how to study. In our sessions, we developed a student success plan to return her to good academic standing. She reflected on her successes and challenges from the last semester.

Adriana informed me that her goal was to return to good academic standing during the current semester, and I reminded her of that goal throughout the semester. She also decided to take a lighter course schedule that included English, math, a community service course, and a course in her major. I recommended that she use additional campus resources, including professors' office hours and the writing center. We developed a time budget to help balance her academics, work, student organizations, and community service. As a result, she earned a GPA that term that resulted in her being in good academic standing for the semester. She eventually graduated from college.

Paul, a White, transfer, electrical engineering student, is another example of an adult learner student who benefited from early academic advising. Paul was making a D and an F in an engineering course and a math course, respectively, when we met near course registration. He admitted to missing course assignments and studying alone. He ended up earning less than a 2.0 GPA for the first term that I met with him. The next semester, we met earlier in the semester. We discussed the courses that he had enjoyed and disliked over the years. We also discussed his past internship, time management, and family issues. He committed to attending professors' office hours, managing time, and engaging in group study. We set academic goals. He wanted to be on Project 4.0—that is, all A's. He ultimately earned four A's and a C that term, so he ended up with a 3.47 GPA, his highest GPA since he entered the university.

In addition to supporting students in one-on-one meetings, an academic advisor can be empowered to encourage and influence administrators to keep students in college when they are experiencing difficulties. When students are not doing particularly well in class and are in jeopardy of being kicked out of college, one of the things that can be done is to use the written record of a student meeting with the academic advisor to actually keep the student in college during the appeals process.

For instance, a Latino male student, Marco, experienced some academic challenges during his first and second years in college. However, because he had met with some campus colleagues and myself, we were able to collectively convince a college dean to keep him on campus. Being an advocate for this student kept him in college. During my career, I've seen the paperwork of academic advisors, academic success coaches, and even graduate advisors being used to help retain college students. So, be encouraged that your voice and efforts can work to facilitate the retention and even graduation of a student or multiple students!

Concluding Summary

To conclude, an academic advisor's role is to help a student navigate through the program curricula. However, to retain and graduate college students, academic advisors must put more time and effort into their students to help facilitate their success beyond advising.

Chapter 3

Academic Success Coach

During my career, I have served as an academic success coach to support college students' persistence, retention, and graduation. An academic success coach ensures that the academic, social, financial, and life issues of college students are addressed. Academic issues that students might face include course rigor, course failure, the need to drop a course after the course deadline, inability to balance academics and other obligations due to lack of time management, and limited study skills. Social issues that college students encounter may include social isolation on campus, lack of access to student organizations, and lack of connection to peers on or off campus.

Financial issues may include limited financial aid, requiring students to work part-time or full-time to pay off their tuition bills. Students might also have an outstanding tuition bill because loans or scholarships do not fully cover their total college expenses. Some students may not have enough funds to cover expenses beyond tuition, such as food, technology, or transportation. Other students may have financial issues due to losing financial aid because of their slow academic progress. Some international students may not be able to pay for college unless they also work.

Life issues that students may face in college can include their parents' divorce, a car accident, domestic disputes, the loss of a loved one, becoming a parent, mental health issues, lack of transportation, or homelessness.

Thus, academic success coaches address the issues that college students endure within and beyond the classroom. How can one person address all of these complicated issues among students? The answer is simple: you need a team of colleagues to support you. Therefore, as an academic success coach, you want to make sure that you have advocates in the form of colleagues in campus offices, such as the Career Services Office, International Student Services, Office of Student Financial Aid, Student Accessibility Services, Tutoring Center, Student Success Center, and Office of Multicultural Student Services.

By having advocates on campus with whom you have formed relationships, it will be easier to refer a student to these colleagues. You can call your colleague up and say that you are referring a student to them, or, if your offices are close, you can walk the student over to your colleague's office to make a formal introduction. You can also monitor a student's progress with your colleague. In addition to student affairs colleagues, it is important to build relationships with academic affairs staff. By doing so, you will be able to get support from these staff if you need to send a student to office hours to see a faculty member, academic advisor, or even an associate dean or dean. In addition, the institutional research team can provide data on students' performance and retention data that you will need for reporting purposes.

One student who needed academic support was Sarah. She was a White woman who had not fully mastered study skills. She also had a learning disability and medical issues. She was brought to the office for early intervention for math and time management. For her success plan, we worked on her time management, and I gave her a time management sheet that we filled out so that she could balance studying and her classes. I gave her a study strategies sheet as well and encouraged her to go to the tutoring center and her math professor's office hours. As a result of my outreach efforts, she successfully passed the math course with a C-.

Similarly, Shannon needed academic support in college. She was an adult learner and a single African American mother raising two adult-aged children. She returned to school after being away from college for more than a decade. She had a learning disability and was on academic probation. In our first meeting, she informed me of having to sign a student academic progress appeal for financial aid. She had signed up for two classes. One of the courses was a computer science class, and she was struggling in that course. I encouraged her to go to tutoring. When that did not fully work for her, I referred her to work one-on-one with her computer science professor. Initially, her professor did not want to help her. However, because I was her advocate, I knew that I had to do something. I reached out to her professor by email to see how we could collaborate to help Shannon learn and be successful in the computer science class. After our conversation, the professor gave her some additional tutoring during his open computer lab hours on Friday evenings and on the weekends. Shannon's computer science professor contacted me via email to give me updates on her progress.

When Shannon fell behind in her other class due to putting so much time into the computer science class, I advocated for her again. I knew the other professor and asked the professor for additional support to set a timeline for Shannon to turn in her missing assignments. The professor worked with us.

Since Shannon worked during the day and had family responsibilities, I usually called her later in the evening to check-in, around 9:30, 10:00, or even 10:30 at night. During these check-ins, I let her know that the computer science professor and her other professor were willing to work with her. During our in-person meetings, I met Shannon wherever she was, including in the building where I was working after hours. She let me know that she was doing well in the computer science class. When we met in the winter term, she informed me that the computer science professor was slipping when it came to providing support. I contacted him again to see if he would provide additional support, and he did.

As a result of my outreach efforts, Shannon earned a 4.0 for that term—she received an A in both of her classes. She was provided the opportunity to learn, which seemed nearly impossible at the beginning of the term. She also worked hard and persevered! The successes of that term increased her confidence in her abilities.

Concluding Summary

To conclude, academic success coaching is a powerful tool to retain and graduate college students. Academic success coaches connect students to multiple resources using their partnerships and personal connections on campus. These include connections to deans, directors, advisors, faculty, and campus staff.

Chapter 4
Mentoring

I was mentored as an undergraduate student, and later, I became a mentor to college students. A mentor is someone who has experienced what a mentee is going through in relation to education, career, or life. A mentor is able to share wisdom with the mentee, wisdom that is invaluable to help the mentee grow or prevent them from making the same mistakes the mentor made in the past. A good mentor wants to see their protégé succeed. An excellent mentor wants their mentee to do better than them in some aspect of life.

Let me introduce you to my first African American woman mentee, Shavon. We met as undergrads during the U of M's Alternative Spring Break, during which we volunteered in Philadelphia. At first, Shavon did not reveal any significant issues during our chats or phone calls. We would check-in with each other via text or messenger platforms. However, when she knew that she wanted to apply for graduate school, she hit a major roadblock. She had a low GPA due to taking up a hard science major, Statistics, in undergrad. I asked her to meet with the chair of a program at a local college she was interested in to see if it was possible to pursue a graduate degree there. The department chair dismissed her and let her know that she was not graduate school material.

However, I knew that her GPA did not reflect her intellectual abilities. I asked her to apply to our alma mater, the U of M, and let her know that I would write her a letter of recommendation. Not only did she get into the U of M's Educational Studies program (more specifically, with a concentration in educational assessment and evaluation), but she also received a $10,000 scholarship. Tragically, she passed away in a freak car accident before finishing her first term at the U of M. She was pursuing her dreams at the point of her untimely death.

Another of my mentees was Candice. She was an African American woman, a nontraditional student whom I met at a program that I facilitated. She became my mentee, and we would often talk in coffee shops about school and life. During one particular chat, she informed me that she was having challenges in school because she felt that she was the "only one" in some of her classes. By "only one," she meant being the only African American woman. She felt isolated. Of course, I shared with her my experiences of being one of the few African Americans on a predominantly White campus in undergrad at the U of M. We discussed ways that she might be able to get involved in student organizations to meet other peers, and she did just that. Prior to her inviting me to her graduation, she told me that had we not had our talk that one evening she might have dropped out of college. That was when I truly realized the power of mentorship. I had contributed to keeping this student in school by listening to her story and sharing my story with her. I knew then that mentoring was one calling in my life, especially mentoring college and graduate students.

An example of a program that I organized and co-chaired for graduate students was the American Educational Studies Association panel entitled

"Mentoring Through Storytelling for Graduate Students: The Road to Academia." During the panel, faculty members (mostly tenured) discussed their knowledge of the tools needed to be successful in academia, including publishing, grant writing, and teaching. I later modified the workshop so that undergraduate students could also benefit from it.

At one institution, we held a program entitled "Fireside Chat: The Past, the Present, the Future: Lessons Learned From Our College Journeys." I was the co-organizer and co-moderator of the panel. I began the program by sharing a personal story with the undergraduates about my paternal grandmother. The summer before college, my grandmother sat me down and admonished me not to get any I's in undergrad. I was offended that she thought so lowly of me, and I didn't even know what an "I" was in undergrad. Of course, later on, I learned that an "I" meant incomplete. My grandmother passed away during my third year of college, but I honored her request and completed college without any incompletes.

However, during my first year of graduate school, I asked my African American male professor and graduate advisor at the time, Dr. Laurence Parker, for an incomplete in one of my courses. I was tired and overwhelmed from the semester. It seemed like my grandmother's presence was in his office at the time, because from the look on his face, I knew I needed to complete that paper and avoid the incomplete. I worked hard to finish that paper for 3 days over a weekend, and I got an A in the class. The lesson I learned was that my grandmother's admonishment about incomplete courses was, in fact, her attempt to mentor me by rescuing me from making the same mistakes that she may have made while in college. Incompletes do not remain incompletes; they turn into F's, which are flunking grades.

During the program, my colleagues, including student affairs staff and faculty members, also told their stories to the undergraduate students to encourage them to remain in college. The majority of the students in the program persisted during their first year of college. Later, I implemented a program called "Mentoring Through Storytelling: The Road to College Graduation." This program provided students with tips from their peers on transitioning to college, financial literacy, and careers.

Concluding Summary

To sum up, mentoring is so influential in the lives of college students. Telling your story in a mentoring program has the power to help retain and graduate college students. Telling college students about your struggles and successes can help them learn how to model the behaviors of a successful college graduate (i.e., the mentor). Thus, mentoring programs are important to have on college campuses, even if they are informal programs like the Mentoring Through Storytelling program that I held on a college campus and at a conference.

Chapter 5

Student Organizations

Student organizations provide students with peer support and reduce feelings of social isolation. Many students meet friends, some even lifelong friends, through these organizations. Organizations can include academic clubs, multicultural student organizations, international student organizations, intramural sports, and even fraternities and sororities. I encourage students to go to the student organization day on their campus to meet new students, who may later become their friends.

In college, I was involved with many student organizations. A few that come to mind are the Black Student Union and Sister2Sister, which was an organization of Black women on campus who volunteered and uplifted one another. The Black Student Union, on the other hand, allowed for more activism on campus to support students. We also put on academic and social programs. By being involved with student organizations, I was never socially isolated in college.

However, social isolation was a common experience among many of my student advisees. For instance, an African college student I advised, Cindy, felt isolated in college. In our conversations, she told me about her interests and her faith. I immediately helped connect her to a Christian organization. She later joined a Christian sorority and the African Student Association. She also needed help finding a job, so I reviewed her resume and cover letter.

Another Black male advisee, Roger, who was a transfer student, became a part of the Black Student Union on campus. The Black Student Union provided him not only with friends but also with an opportunity to be on the leadership team. Roger and I spoke about some of his academic challenges. I remember him telling me that he was dropping out of college, but I encouraged him to stay. The notion of dropping out of college was not foreign to him because his mother had done so. The idea of graduating may have been scary for Roger. Roger decided to only take off the summer semester. Later, he graduated from college with his bachelor's degree.

A final example is Douglas, a Black engineering student. He was on the leadership team of the National Society of Black Engineers but was not doing well in some of his classes. I brought him in to meet with me during an advising session. We talked about his challenges, and some were personal in nature. He had trouble balancing work and school. For his success plan, we developed a time budget so that he would have time to study, engage in student organizations, and work. I also gave him a study strategies sheet based on the different learning styles (e.g., auditory, kinesthetic, visual). Douglas passed all of his classes that semester. He finished college and earned his bachelor's degree in electrical engineering.

Concluding Summary

To sum up, student organizations play a significant role in reducing social isolation in college. However, being a part of student organizations is not enough to retain and graduate college students. Students still need support and encouragement to help them to persist in their studies and graduate from college.

Chapter 6
Employment Opportunities

In college, to retain and graduate students, it is important to connect them to employment opportunities. On-campus employment is especially well suited for students because there is usually a restriction on the number of hours that a student can work. Work-study jobs are also great because they allow students to work part-time so that they can still be fully engaged in their academics. Off-campus jobs are not as ideal for students because students may decide to work full-time, which may negatively impact their grades if they are unable to balance work with their academics. Students who work off-campus or full-time may not be able to go to professors' office hours or take advantage of the benefits of being on a college campus, like going to tutoring or meeting with their peers. These students, especially adult learners, are at-risk of leaving school if they do not have a connection to campus besides attending classes.

At one of the college campuses where I worked, there was a need for providing paid internships to college students through the Career Services Office. However, students were unaware of those paid internships, so I began to build a partnership with the Career Services Office. I sent students there to interview for and obtain internships. For instance, an Asian student, Ian, was in need of a paid internship for his particular major, so I connected him to the Career Services Office. He then interviewed for a couple of positions and landed a job.

Besides the Career Services Office, I have sent students to on-campus career fairs to meet with prospective employers. I've even collected the brochures and business cards of prospective employers to give students who may have been like me in college and did not know that going to a career fair was an option as a first-generation college student.

Another way to obtain work during college is to join a summer program, such as the McNair Scholars Program, to obtain a research position. An African woman, Angela, who was a psychology major with a minor in chemistry was a part of the McNair Scholars Program. She began working on a research project in a research lab on campus with me. I mentored her through the writing process. She wrote an article-length paper on health in African American communities. She later traveled with her peers to conferences, including a McNair Research conference, and presented her scholarship at the McNair Research conference on campus. After graduating from college, she went to medical school. We kept in contact, and I co-wrote a recommendation letter for a medical school summer program, which she got into. She graduated from medical school in 2016.

Concluding Summary

To conclude, employment is good for students. It provides them with experiences of the real world. But employment can hinder students from persisting in college due to the challenge of balancing work and studies. Although I recommend part-time employment, some students have to work full-time because they have exhausted all of their financial resources. However, those students can work with their academic success coaches or a student success center to develop plans to succeed by balancing work and academics.

Chapter 7

Technology

On college campuses, technology is crucial for implementing a successful student retention program. I've used programs, including the Degree Audit Reporting System (DARS) at the University of Illinois, to help students find classes to register for each term. However, students registering for classes in the banner system need all of their holds to be cleared, including financial and academic holds, in order to register for classes each term.

Unlike the technology available at the University of Illinois, Wayne State University had a more robust system for tracking student success. The system that we used was called the Student Tracking Advising Retention System (STARS). STARS told us if students had holds on their accounts; it also provided information on students' current curricula and students' GPAs each term. We were also able to download student data on grades and enrollment in Microsoft Excel. This was particularly helpful when I had to run reports for my department to monitor student progress each term. Student advising meeting notes were also able to be input into the STARS database.

Finally, at Indiana University South Bend, we used the Student Information System, which included students' grades, course registration, and holds and information about their academic advisor, financial aid advisor, 21st Century Scholar advisor, and even student success coach. Adrx was a technology tool that allowed us to see each student's schedule and GPA and let us enter student notes for advising meetings.

Concluding Summary

To sum up, technology is critical to track students' GPAs and take notes on their issues in case a staff member or administrator on campus needs to advocate for a student who is in jeopardy of flunking out of college. Thus, the technological "paper trail" can be helpful in retaining students. Technology also allows staff and administrators to view the case notes left by other staff (if the notes are public information), which is helpful in case of a student audit and to share information, especially if a staff member leaves the university.

Chapter 8
Creating a Paper Trail and Report Writing

To effectively retain and graduate college students, it is important to track their successes and failures by creating a paper trail and writing reports. Every school keeps academic records of students' grade point averages (GPAs), including incompletes and withdrawals from coursework. Thus, this is an easy way to track students' academic successes and failures, but there is more you can do beyond the school's system.

What might be some student successes that you can celebrate? You can celebrate them achieving honors, winning an award, or doing well on a quiz or an exam. Other accolades might be for obtaining an internship, job, or leadership position in a student organization. These praises go a long way to support a student's efforts to be successful within and beyond the classroom.

What might be some challenges to document? If a student has dealt with adversity (e.g., death, domestic violence, verbal abuse, trauma, homelessness, gun violence, lack of transportation, lack of child care) or financial distress, then it is important to document those experiences in your case notes or a private paper file. These files will be particularly helpful if that student needs an advocate.

You might wonder why students reveal their stories of trials and even tragedies to a success coach or an academic advisor like me. I found that students shared these experiences because they felt comfortable around me. Often, I engaged in real talk or was so authentic that they let their guard down, which allowed them to be their "real" selves around me. When meeting with students, I engaged in a strategic approach that I call *Real Outreach*, which is a retention and graduation model. I will discuss this model in more detail in Chapter 9.

When tracking student progress, you can document students' successes and failures using a paper trail with paper files. You can also track students' successes and failures in a Microsoft Excel database or a Microsoft Word document. If available at your school, you can also document students' progress in public or private notes in a web-based database.

Finally, once you track students' successes and failures, it is important to form these notes into a final report. You should document how many times you met with the student during the semester and the on-campus and off-campus resources that you gave to the student. You should follow up with the student to see if they actually used those on-campus and off-campus resources and document that as well. You also want to document students' successes and failures and whether you would support them if they had an academic audit at the end of the term. This is particularly helpful for students who may be in jeopardy of flunking out of college. If the students had life issues and met with a staff member or other campus employees to address those issues, then that can be used as evidence that those students should be given another chance at the university. As a staff member, you should also document how many students you helped retain each semester so that you can show administrators how you are pushing the needle toward supporting student persistence, retention, and graduation!

Concluding Summary

To conclude, tracking students' successes and failures is key to the retention and graduation of college students because you are making a paper trail that may be useful in the future. Students may be in jeopardy of failing or may have failed a semester for a valid reason. If those students are making progress by meeting with an academic advisor or academic success coach or using other campus resources, then it might be worthwhile for institutions to consider working with those students rather than pushing them out of college, which will be a negative hit on the institution's overall retention and graduation statistics.

Chapter 9

Real Outreach:
A Successful Student Retention and Graduation Model

During my career, to retain and graduate as many at-risk students as I have, I must have done something right. I use a strategic approach to facilitate the persistence, retention, and graduation of students who are at-risk of leaving college due to poor academics, social isolation, finances, and life issues. The approach involves having a care team of supportive colleagues on campus. I call this strategic approach Real Outreach. Real Outreach is an acronym that I will define later in this chapter. A visualization of the Real Outreach retention and graduation model is provided in Figure 1.

Figure 1: Real Outreach: A Student Retention and Graduation Model

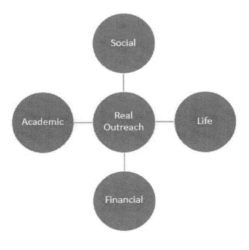

As shown in Figure 1, Real Outreach addresses college students' academic, social, financial, and life issues that are barriers to their persistence, retention, and graduation. Once these barriers are addressed by a caring team of campus professionals, college students are in a better position not only to be retained but also to persist each term and eventually graduate from college.

Some students come to college confused with questions that they may not even know how to ask a faculty member, staff, or administrator, especially if they are first-generation college students. Other students have financial issues and need to work part-time or full-time. In some cases, their scholarships and loans have run out due to academic failure. Some students not only fail exams and quizzes but fail courses and even flunk out of school. Others struggle to balance being a student with family responsibilities and community obligations.

The "Real" in the Real Outreach Student Retention and Graduation Model

The "real" in the Real Outreach retention and graduation model stands for resiliency, empathy, approachability, and listening.

Resiliency

In my career, I have retained and graduated many college students and mentees by teaching them how to be resilient and to continue to stick to their studies despite obstacles, such as academic, financial, social, or life issues. Walsh (1998) defines resilience as "the capacity to rebound from adversity strengthened and more resourceful" (p. 4). The framework of resiliency "is based on the conviction that both individual and family strength can be forged through collaborative efforts to deal with sudden crisis or prolonged adversity" (Walsh, 1998, p. 3).

I want to provide an example of how I taught resiliency to a college student. One of my advisees was an African American woman named Benita. Her financial aid was delayed because she turned in the Free Application for Federal Student Aid (FAFSA) late. With support from the Office of Student Financial Aid, we found out that she was missing the Master Promissory Note for her loans, so she turned in that paperwork along with her parents' signatures for funding. Throughout the semester, I encouraged Benita to stay focused on her academics, be patient, and worry less about the finances because everything would work out. She shared books with peers and obtained books from the library and her instructors. As a result of meeting with Benita and checking on her coursework and financial aid, she ended up with a 3.9 GPA during her first semester in college. Her financial aid in the form of scholarships and loans came through at the end of the semester, too.

Empathy

In my career and life, I've learned that having empathy means being able to walk a day in someone else's shoes. When you are empathetic, you are able to understand, to a certain extent, where your student has been. You can also understand their moments of pain and pride.

As one example during my career, I was able to show empathy to an African American student named Laura. Laura informed me that she would be walking down the graduation stage in May, even though she was told that she would not earn her degree until the summer of that year. I told her that she should hold her head up high and walk down that graduation stage proud of her accomplishment. She, too, was a first-generation college student. I not only shared with her that I was a first-generation college student, but I also revealed to her that I understood her situation because I had done the same thing for my doctoral graduation. I walked in May even though I received my degree in August of that year. Tears rolled down her face as she realized that I fully understood her pain and the level of embarrassment that she felt walking down the graduation stage without getting a degree. Some students walk for graduation and never get their degrees. However, Laura was not one of those students; she finished her degree in the summer.

Approachability

Through trial and error, I have learned that it is important for college students to feel comfortable approaching staff. Students have to feel comfortable talking with staff members about their problems. According to Ginsberg (2005), being approachable means (a) "being ready to engage" (p. 21); (b) "being accessible and easy to deal with" (p. 38); (c) being "friendly and ready to listen and help"; and (d) being "easy to meet, converse, and do business with" (p. 140).

Implementing an "open door policy" lets college students know that they can approach you when the door is open. A closed door means the opposite—"do not disturb." Bolton (1979) provides more details regarding being approachable with your body language and was one of the first to coin the term *door openers*. He states that door openers are "a description of the other person's body language" (p. 41). We can verbally say "please go on", or "I'm interested in what you are saying" (p. 41). We can also be silent and provide "the other person time to decide whether to talk and/or what he wants to say" (p. 41). Finally, we can be attending with our body language, namely with our eyes and posture, which "demonstrates [our] interest in and concern for the other person" (p. 41).

In my career, I've learned that positive body language involves eye contact, good posture, leaning forward to show that you are interested, listening to the conversation, and nodding your head and smiling. Regarding being perceived as approachable, sometimes your nonverbal actions speak louder than words.

Listening

I have found that listening to your college students' concerns is so important if you want to effectively retain and graduate them in a timely manner. Bolton (1979) states that "one of the primary tasks of a listener is to stay out of the other's way so that the listener can discover how the speaker views the situation" (p. 40). However, what becomes problematic in most conversations is that "the average 'listener' interrupts and diverts the speaker by asking many questions or making many statements" (Bolton, 1979, p. 40).

Active listening is important so that you are able to fully understand your student. According to Grande (2020), "active listening is a way of listening that involves the full attention to what is being said for the primary purpose of understanding the speaker" (p. 1). To be an active listener, a person should "listen without making judgements or taking a position on an issue" (p. 1). Other ways to be an active listener are to "show that your attention is focused. [You should] make eye contact [and] lean in towards the speaker when your interest peaks" (p.1). Grande also states to "repeat what you have heard to check for accuracy" (p. 1). Finally, Grande says to "ask questions as needed when you don't understand what the speaker is trying to communicate" (p. 1).

Reflective listening is another approach to use to retain college students. In academic advising and academic success coaching, I have found myself engaging in reflective listening. According to Bolton (1979), reflective listening involves the following: (a) mirroring, in which "the listener restates the feelings and/or content of what the speaker has communicated and does so in a way that communicates understanding and acceptance" (p. 50); (b) paraphrasing, which consists of a "concise response to the speaker which states the essence of the other's content in the listener's words" (p. 51); (c) reflecting feeling, which is "mirroring back to the speaker, in succinct statements, the emotions which he is communicating" (p. 52); (d) hearing feelings, which is done when one "read[s] the emotions of others" (p. 54); and (e) listening for feeling words, that is, "identify[ing] the verbally expressed feelings in conversations" (p. 55). Bolton sums up listening by stating that listening involves being present with your mind, body, and even gestures.

An example of a student I listened to was Allison. Allison was a White woman who left the university due to medical issues. She began the university as an honor student. However, as an engineering student, she was in academic jeopardy due to her poor academic performance. She informed me that she was on medical

48

withdrawal due to her cancer treatment. I told her that I understood what she was going through and shared with her that I had family members who had cancer, so I understood a bit of what she was going through. I remember that tears rolled down her face. In the end, she enrolled in a math class. Cases like Allison's require extra care, empathy, and a listening ear.

The "Outreach" in the Real Outreach Student Retention and Graduation Model

The "outreach" part of the Real Outreach student retention and graduation model stands for observations, understanding, trust, resources and referrals, encouragement, advocate, caring and compassionate customer service, and hospitality.

Observations

During my career, I had to be very observant of my students in the office. I had to observe their behaviors, emotions, and even their facial expressions. By observing their nonverbal (body language) and verbal cues, I was able to ascertain whether or not they wanted to meet with me. Most students were happy to meet with me. However, other students who were on or headed toward academic probation were more hesitant to meet with me, and it was evident. However, I turned some of those frowns into smiles by the end of our meetings.

Understanding

I've learned that understanding a student's concerns is key to addressing them in order to effectively retain and graduate that student from college. I also learned that by fully understanding and answering students' questions and concerns, they would come back for more meetings with me. By trying to truly understand my students, I was on the pathway to providing good customer service. According to Evenson (2012), "the only way to give truly great [customer] service is first to understand what the customer wants" (p. 53). She further states: "satisfy each customer and you improve your chances they will come back" (p. 53).

Carlaw and Deming (1999) state that you should confirm your understanding of a person. First, you should "use a confirming statement," such as "let me confirm" (p. 131). Second, you should "summarize the facts" (p. 131). Third, you should "ask if your understanding is correct" (p. 131) by asking a question such as, "Did I get that right?" Finally, a person should "clarify understandings (if necessary)" (p. 131).

Trust

In my mentoring experiences and career, mentees and college students have learned to trust me because of my approach to being honest with them. I've shared my personal stories with some of my college students and definitely my mentees. I also allow my college students and mentees to be their authentic selves with me. Once they revealed their deep personal stories of trials and tragedies to me, I knew that they really trusted me, as some were even stories they had never shared with another adult.

Resources/Referrals

Often, students run into obstacles with regards to academics, finances, social issues, and life issues. However, they cannot see what I see, which is them at the finish line, namely graduation! Not only have I referred students to on-campus and off-campus resources, but I have also made referrals to my network of colleagues inside and outside of the university. I learned to give students accurate information. If I did not know the answer, then I let students know that I would have the information for them by the next time we met or that I would send it to them in an email if that was their preferred method of contact.

Encouragement

As a mentor, academic advisor, and academic success coach, I've always encouraged my mentees and college students. By encouragement, I mean giving them the support and confidence to let them know that they can succeed. Liz was a Latina, nontraditional student who had a son while in college. She was a part of one of my programs and became my mentee. I met her where she was, which was usually at the bookstore where she worked. We talked about academics and her family. I always encouraged Liz to get her degree even when it seemed like it was impossible. She succeeded and graduated with her bachelor's degree. As with Liz, I encourage all of my mentees and college students to never quit and to dream big!

Advocate

I am my mentees' and college students' biggest advocate! I am there to support them through academic, financial, social, and life issues. I've had phone triages with students and their financial aid advisors to discuss financial aid issues. I've advocated for students' professors to work with students to turn in missing assignments when I knew the students had life issues. I have convinced deans to keep students in the university who should have been kicked out due to their academic progress. I have persuaded college administrators to give funds to students who lacked the money to pay their tuition bills.

I've worked with academic advisors as well to get students into classes that they may have been barred from due to their academic standing. As an academic success coach, I have even advised students to drop classes as needed. I have attended students' meetings (by phone or in person) with other staff members to ask questions on their behalf, if needed. Even though I was an advocate for these students, I empowered them to make their own decisions.

Caring and Compassionate Customer Service

Some of our college students are suffering academically, financially, socially, or with life's issues. In my career, I've learned that caring and compassionate customer service helps retain and graduate college students. The framework of interpersonal caring dictates that "the person who is caring is concerned about, and willing to attempt to meet the physical, psychological, and academic needs of the individual for [whom] that person is caring" (Siddle Walker & Tompkins, 2004, p. 79). Glassman and Kates (1990) state that "caring for others occurs when members respond to each other's hurts, discomforts, satisfactions, concerns, and fears" (p. 28).

In addition to caring, compassion is being sympathetic to someone facing misfortune and desiring to take action to alleviate that person's suffering. Besides being compassionate, it is important to build relationships with customers, who are our students and mentees in higher education. Evenson (2012) states that we can build relationships by establishing rapport; to do this, we should "be friendly, interested in their needs, considerate of their feelings, listen, and be relatable" (pp. 74–75). We can also "interact positive[ly] with customers [by being] helpful, committed, credible, [and] a problem solver" (pp. 77–78). We can be helpful by "identifying the customer's needs"; we can ask "questions, determine their needs, provide solutions to address their needs [and] handle objections and opposition" (pp. 79–80). Finally, we can "make the customer feel valued [by going] the extra mile to serve them, validate their decisions, [and have them] leave on a positive note" (p. 82).

Charmaine is an example of a student to whom I provided caring and compassionate customer service in college. She was an African American student with a disability. We had an established relationship, as we had met during her freshman year. She struggled academically and financially during her sophomore year of college. I not only cared for her, but I sympathized with her because I felt her pain. I even told her about the trials and tribulations of my financial distress during my sophomore year of college, which appeared to encourage her. She always seemed to do well during the beginning of the term, yet by the midterm, her grades declined. We met every 2 to 3 weeks to check-in and discuss her academic, social, financial, and life issues. She was vulnerable with me, which meant that she trusted me to share her concerns.

At midterm, when her grades slipped, she told me that she had failed some exams. As her academic success coach, I held her accountable by checking in. I observed that she lacked motivation and drive. I encouraged her to stick with college despite these obstacles.

Recommendations that I gave her for success included attending the professor's office hours to seek support, going to the tutoring center, working with peers during group projects, and paying down the tuition bill. As a result of mentorship and academic success coaching, she earned a 3.0 GPA for that semester. She graduated from college with her bachelor's degree as well.

Hospitality

The final component of the Real Outreach student retention and graduation model is hospitality. I've learned that the art of providing hospitality is important to retaining and graduating students. As an institution, you want to create a "home away from home" for your students. Other ways to display hospitality include having a warm and pleasant demeanor and having candy or even tissues in the office to offer students. Offering programs that involve food and fellowship also provides students with a "southern hospitality" that makes them feel welcomed at a university.

Concluding Summary

To conclude, as you build your retention program, you need to think about addressing the academic, social, financial, and life issues of college students as a collective through the use of a care team on campus. I implore you to use the Real Outreach retention model. I am confident that the model works because I've had excellent results using this model in retaining and graduating students who were otherwise on the path to dropping out of college.

Chapter 10
Conclusion

To retain and graduate college students, it is important to collectively support these students. This may be through academic advisors, academic success coaches, or even mentors who develop partnerships on campus with academic affairs, student affairs, enrollment services, and the institutional research team. The retention and graduation of college students rarely happens in a silo. Thus, I implore your institution to work collectively as a team to support students' success! Keeping a paper trail and writing reports will be important to retain students who are especially at-risk for dropping out of school due to academic, financial, social, or life issues.

Your documentation will be helpful if a student goes up for an academic audit to show that the student used campus resources to attempt to improve their progress. That student may be one that a dean decides to give a second or even third chance to remain in college, rather than kicking the student out, which will negatively impact the institution's retention and graduation statistics. Finally, developing or investing in a student retention and graduation model like Real Outreach will produce high returns on your investment. I am confident that my strategic approach to college student retention and graduation works because I have retained and graduated hundreds of students who might have never graduated without my support.

References

Bolton, R. (1979). *People skills: How to assert yourself, listen to others, and resolve conflicts.* New York: Simon & Schuster.

Carlaw, P., & Deming, V. K. (1999). The *big book of customer service training games.* New York: McGraw-Hill.

Evenson, R. (2012). *Powerful phrases for effective customer service: Over 700 ready-to-use phrases and scripts that really get results.* New York: American Management Association.

Ginsberg, S. (2005). *The power of approachability.* Scott Ginsburg.

Glassman, U., & Kates, L. (1990). *Group work: A humanistic approach.* Thousand Oaks: Sage Publications.

Grande, D. (2020, June 2). Active listening skills: Why active listening is important, and how to do it. *Psychology Today.* https://www.psychologytoday.com/us/blog/in-it-together/202006/active-listening-skills

Siddle Walker, V., & Tompkins, R. H. (2004). Caring in the Past: The case of southern segregated African American schools." In V. Siddle Walker & J.R. Snarey (Eds.), Racing moral formation: African American perspectives on care and justice (pp. 77–92). New York: Teachers College Press.

Walsh, F. (1998). *Strengthening family resilience.* New York, NY: Guilford Press.

Biography

Dr. Ezella McPherson is an African American woman first-generation college graduate and a college student retention expert. She has mentored, retained, and graduated hundreds of students by teaching them the art of resiliency. She has worked at multiple higher education institutions, where she has increased college student enrollment, retention, and graduation rates. She taught a course on retaining at-risk collegians at Eastern Michigan University. She has published and presented on college student persistence, retention, and graduation of African American women, minority students, and science, technology, engineering, and math (STEM) students. She earned her bachelor's degree from the University of Michigan–Ann Arbor and her master's and doctorate degrees in educational policy studies from the University of Illinois at Urbana-Champaign. If you'd like to contact Dr. McPherson regarding consulting work, a training, or a speaking engagement, she can be reached via email at emcpher2@gmail.com.

Made in the USA
Columbia, SC
09 November 2024

45887968R00037